Beyond The Bullshit: Cipher's Life Hacks for Gen Z

Orange Books Publication

1st Floor, Rajhans Arcade, Mall Road, Kohka, Bhilai, Chhattisgarh 490020
Website: **www.orangebooks.in**

© Copyright, 2025, Author

All rights reserved. No part of this book may be reproduced, stored in a retrieval system, or transmitted, in any form by any means, electronic, mechanical, magnetic, optical, chemical, manual, photocopying, recording or otherwise, without the prior written consent of its writer.

First Edition, 2025

ISBN: 978-93-6554-428-2

BEYOND
—— THE ——
BULLSHIT
CIPHER'S LIFE HACKS FOR GEN Z

CIPHER

Practical Wisdom For Those Fed Up With
Self-Help Sugar Highs

Orange Books Publication
www.orangebooks.in

Index

1. **Purpose Of The Book** 1
2. **Must Learn Basics** 3
   Crowd Is Always Wrong 3
   Law Of Diminishing Utility/Efficiency 6
   Law Of Pendulum 8
   Nature Always Seeks Balance 8
   Case Study: My Fight Against Water Phobia 9
3. **The 33.33% Rule** 12
   You Cannot Please Everyone 12
   The Celebrity Trap 14
   The Risk Of Bending Backwards 15
   Lesson From Mahabharat 16
4. **Understanding Life's Assertions** 20
   Mother Nature Is Capitalist 20
   Excellence Thrives In Any Case 22
   There Is No Such Thing As "Struggle" 24
   There Is No Such Thing As "Optimum Or
   Ideal Life" 26
   The Desired Result Isn't Guaranteed 29
   There Is No Such Thing As "Retirement" 31

5. Mindset And Perspective 38
- You And Your Problems Are Not Special 38
- Embracing Tunnel Vision 41
- Broken Window Fallacy Of Life And Drama Triangle 43
- Sunk Cost Fallacy 46
- The "Listen To Your Heart" Bullshit 47
- The Misleading Dropout By Choice Narrative 49

6. Acceptance And Growth 51
- Accepting Limitations 51
- Survival Mechanism Kicks In As We Accept Mistakes 53
- Understanding Luck And Skill 56

7. Practical Guidance 58
- The Key To Success Is "Repetitive 'Submaximal' Effort" 58
- Tracking Saturn For Expectations Management 61
- Don't Sell 62
- Beware Of Dark Psychology 65
- Promises Are Cool But Complicate Life 69
- The Real Spirituality 71

1. Purpose Of The Book

Hey there, Amigo. Welcome to "Beyond the Bullshit: Cipher's Life Hacks for Gen Z." This book is a culmination of my [Cipher's] experiences, insights, and the lessons I've learned along the way. In a world swarming with folks striving for above-average achievements, Cipher is your friendly neighbourhood everyman, navigating life's complexities and hustling to succeed in his endeavors.

In this era of social media highlights and curated perfection, it's all too easy to feel like you're falling behind or that everyone else has it all figured out. As an average Joe who's navigated the trenches, Cipher can assure you that the journey to achieving above average is often messy, fraught with uncertainties, and plagued by misconceptions.

Fear not; this book is now your typical positive thinking manual filled with mantras and cringeworthy exercises where you stand in front of the mirror shouting, "I can win." It's a candid exploration of what it means to navigate life as part of Generation Z. We'll tackle the tough stuff—the realities that many shy away from discussing. From understanding the fickle nature of our desires to recognizing that very few things in life come without effort and sacrifice, we'll uncover the essential truths that can help you chart your own path.

We'll dive into analogies from the world of economics and absolute sciences to shed light on why sometimes less really is more, and the importance of acceptance in the face of challenges. Cipher shares insights on how to avoid falling for flashy promises and how to cultivate a mindset that fosters growth and resilience. You see, it's not about being extraordinary; it's about being real. It's about learning to accept our flaws and limitations while striving for improvement.

But take note of this scoop: Cipher is not a trained life coach or psychiatrist, but an ordinary guy sharing his journey, packed with titbits of intelligence picked up from 40 years of being a living, breathing entity on this tough planet. So, you may notice that the structure of this book is not as slick and polished as those authored by seasoned psychology experts or writers.

That said, the insights presented in this book are relatable and practical, grounded in the reality of everyday struggles, and backed with analogies cutting across disciplines with an aim to set you on the right path away from the ill trappings of the human mind.

So, grab a cup of coffee or your favourite beverage, and let's embark on this journey together! This book is for the dreamers, the hustlers, and anyone willing to look beyond the hype to uncover the truths that can lead us to a more fulfilling life. The book will give you perspectives you haven't yet considered. Welcome aboard!

2. Must Learn Basics

Getting a grip on the basics is a game-changer when it comes to levelling up in life. Think of a house without a decent foundation it just doesn't work, right? It's the same with personal growth.

In this first chapter, we're diving into four super essential principles: the Crowd is Always Wrong, the Law of Diminishing Returns, the Law of Pendulum, and Nature's Law of Balance. Now, I am not just throwing around jargon. These practical ideas will genuinely shift your perspective to make smart decisions and address life issues.

Before we look at a real-life example of how to apply these insights to tackle issues, let's take a moment to get to know each individually. It will make it easier to see how they connect, guiding you along a more straightforward path to overcome whatever issues you face. Let's go.

The crowd is always wrong
American poet and novelist Charles Bukowski said it best: "The masses are always wrong - Wisdom is doing everything the crowd does not do. All you do is reverse the totality of their learning and you have the heaven they're looking for."

One of the simplest ways to sidestep life's pitfalls is to take a moment to evaluate whether your thoughts or plans align with the popular sentiment. If they do, there's a good chance you might be on the wrong path. In such cases, looking in the opposite or different directions for solutions can be helpful. Often, the best insights come from perspectives that aren't widely accepted or popular. (Note that popular opinions backed by absolute sciences should be followed to a tee.)

After spending over a decade in the world of financial markets, a vast sea of human emotions, I can't emphasize enough how crucial it is to look past what the crowd is doing. There are countless examples of popular opinion gone wrong, leading to massive wealth destruction. The blind faith that real estate prices can never go down set the stage for the 2008 crash. The crypto market goes through phases of euphoria marked by crowd sentiment leaning too bullish, followed by a crash. A similar thing happened with tech stocks after the Dot com bubble burst in 2000.

Much more serious examples of crowd sentiment leading to disastrous outcomes include the rise of dictators like Adolf Hitler in Germany and Benito Mussolini in Italy, the perennial democratic instability and frequent authoritative martial law impositions in Pakistan, the country's obsession with Kashmir at the behest of economic stability and erstwhile McCarthyism in the United States.

You can find plenty of examples of the crowd being wrong in academia. Take the pattern where a new course suddenly gets all the hype and becomes the must-have degree. At first, it's exciting; students flock to enroll, and universities scrabble to create programs. But here's the catch: once the crowd is all in on a course, that's usually when you've hit the peak. When everyone jumps on the bandwagon, it signals that the course has reached its height of popularity. After that, it's often a downhill slide.

AI-generated image representing Bukoswki's quote. (Google Gemini)

This is exactly what happened with the MBA degree in India between 2000 and 2006. During that time, an MBA became the golden ticket for job seekers, and everyone wanted to get in on the action. Universities and business schools started popping up everywhere, churning out so-called management experts.

By 2006-07, the crowd was convinced that MBA was a ticket to millions if not billions and sure enough the degree lost its charm immediately in the subsequent years. I happened to be one of those who got carried away by the popular sentiment and took my two-year MBA in 2007. I don't want to go into details of what happened later when I stepped into the job market!

Law of diminishing utility/efficiency

This one might ring a bell with students of economics. The law of diminishing utility (you can call it diminishing returns/efficiency) states that during the course of consumption, as more and more units of goods or services are consumed, every successive unit gives utility with a diminishing rate.

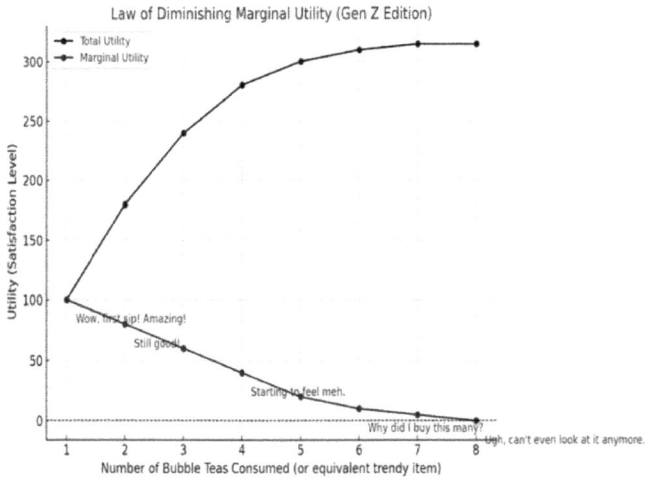

Law of DMU (ChatGPT)

The pictorial representation shows how the total utility or satisfaction derived tops and turns lower with marginal utility dropping to zero, the so-called puking stage. Economists assume units are consumed without a break, just as you SIMP 24/7 for your crush! Marginal utility refers to satisfaction generated by an additional unit of goods or services consumed.

Picture this: You have been pouring your heart and soul into winning over your crush. You are available 24/7, texting and calling, and within a stone's throw, thinking you are scoring major points. But here is the catch: your perennial availability makes you less unique to your love interest and takes you closer to that feared "friend-zoned" status.

Your constant presence diminishes your perceived value or attractiveness, and the utility your crush derives from you dips into negative territory. Eventually, you will be a guest at your crush's wedding. That's the law of diminishing marginal utility, my friend.

An example can be found in thermodynamics, especially in the context of heat transfer in a cooling system. In an air conditioning unit, the rate of heat transfer is tied to the temperature difference between the inside of a room and the outside environment.

Initially, the system quickly removes the heat from the room as the temperature difference is significant. However, as the room cools and the temperature difference narrows, the heat transfer rate decreases, representing the diminishing driving force (the temperature gradient) for heat flow. Eventually, as equilibrium nears, the cooling effect becomes less effective in the form of diminishing returns.

Almost every problem in our lives can be traced to the law of DMU.

Law of pendulum

A pendulum that swings to one extreme will swing to the other extreme before settling at the center. At extremes, it has maximum potential energy. It's a metaphor for understanding life cycles and the natural ebb and flow we experience in various aspects of our lives.

Life is never straight and an equilibrium or the center is reached only on death. The Law of Pendulum suggests that whatever is happening in your life, whether it's happiness, success, failure, or stress, will eventually swing back in the opposite direction.

Nature always seeks balance

Nature balances itself through what is known as the law of balance. It says that nature continually works to restore equilibrium over time, smoothing out the fluctuations between extremes highlighted by the Law of Pendulum.

Keeping this law in mind will ensure you take steps to improve your situation and keep faith that the pendulum will swing to the other extreme, balancing out the tough times you face with good ones.

So, the next time you set out to tackle your challenges, remember to trust the process because it will yield results. The Law of the Pendulum and nature's ability to find balance remind us that tough times don't last forever. If we take the right steps, the sun will shine bright again. It's clear that it's not just about positive affirmations magically solving everything!

Case study: my fight against water phobia

Now that you've got a good grasp of these concepts, let's talk about how they can help tackle personal issues, using a story from my own life.

I used to have a crippling phobia of water. My heart would race, and I would scream and cry just being in the swimming pool under the watchful eyes of my family. By the time I turned 14, I felt like overcoming this fear was impossible.

That's when my maternal uncle, a surgeon, stepped in. He went against what many well-meaning but overprotective family members advised – telling me to stay away from water – and instead encouraged me to face my fear. It's a great example of the idea that the **crowd is often wrong**; in this case, I was part of that crowd, too, as my phobia represented a form of irrationality that was fuelled by fear.

So, I began accompanying him to the swimming pool regularly. At first, all he asked me to do was sit on the pool deck—nothing more. As days went by, the **law of DMU kicked in**, and the ability of water to scare the shit out of me diminished with each passing day.

After a couple of weeks, I felt ready to get in the water. I started by standing in the shallow end, around 3-4 feet deep, with lifeguards warned against forcing me into the deep end. I spent weeks doing this, and the DMU continued to work its magic; gradually, my phobia faded.

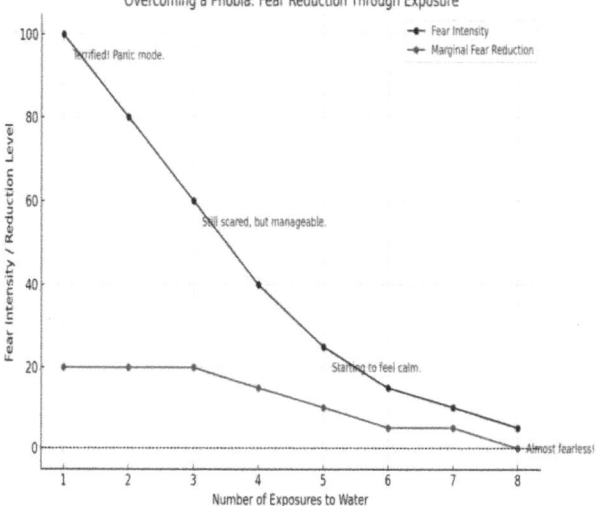

The graph shows the phobia diminished with the increase in the number of exposures to water. (Source: ChatGPT)

As the **law of the pendulum** suggests, my phobia—representing the negative extreme—ultimately swung to the opposite extreme of optimism and confidence, allowing **nature to restore balance** within me. With enough practice, my phobia dissipated, and in two months, I competed in a novice freestyle race, where I proudly secured second place.

Now, I can dive, swim underwater, and enjoy my time there. It's important to note that while I'm still aware of the dangers associated with water – after all, it's healthy to have a bit of caution – my phobia is wholly gone.

I encourage you to assess your situations through the lens of these laws. Whether you're facing a plateau in your career or workouts, wondering why that pre-workout you used to rely on no longer provides stimulus, or feeling like you've been friend-zoned by your social circle, these principles can guide you toward finding balance.

Here are the steps to follow

1. **Write Down Your Problem**: Take a moment to articulate the issue, put it down on paper to understand it better, and find a logical starting point for finding solutions.

2. **Check Popular Sentiment:** Evaluate the general consensus or popular opinion regarding your problem. This could be family, friends, or even articles and social media advice.

3. **Look where the crowd is not looking**: Once you've identified the popular sentiment, consider taking a different or opposite approach.

4. **Have Faith in the Process**: Just as nature strives for balance and the pendulum swings to the other extreme, your efforts toward finding a solution will work and lead to positive changes.

Note that I am not a trained psychiatrist, and the strategies discussed here are based solely on my personal experience. Caution is advised when applying these steps.

3. The 33.33% Rule

My friend's teen sister was in a complete meltdown mode the other day. She had spent hours creating a perfect Instagram post that sported a cool caption and trendy vibe with an aesthetically pleasing location. Still, instead of going viral, the post got just a handful of likes, and, to her dismay, someone commented, this outfit is so basic. She was devastated and started second-guessing herself, thinking she was probably not cool or interesting enough.

That incident took me back to a principle I developed while dealing with social media trolls over my articles about the financial markets. My desire to please everyone made me feel incredibly stressed, which is when I came up with the 33.33% rule, which says that at a given point in time, for every person who likes you, there will be someone who dislikes you, and a third group simply won't care about you at all. It's rooted in the simple truth that nature always seeks balance.

You cannot please everyone

The essence of the rule is that trying to win over everyone is a trap so many of us fall into, especially in the age of social media and attention economy, where everyone is chasing likes, comments and validation. It's emotionally draining and often leads you.

Beyond The Bullshit: Cipher's Life Hacks for Gen Z

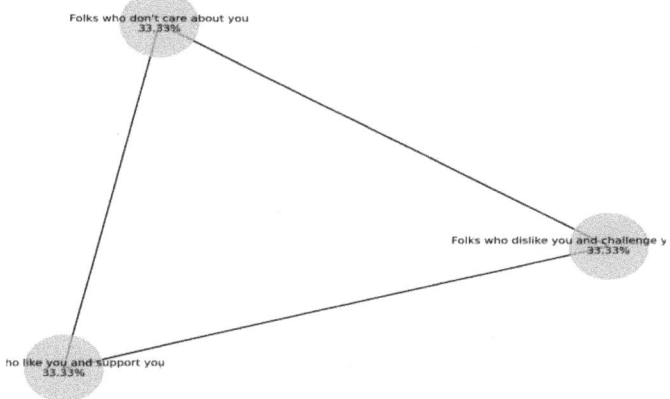

The graph illustrates the distribution of people in your life, categorized into those who like and support you, those who dislike and challenge you, and those who are indifferent. Each category represents 33.33% of the people in your life. (Google Gemini)

to a path where you end up bending backwards and validating folks that do not really deserve and are not qualified for your validation.

Here is why winning over everyone is impossible:

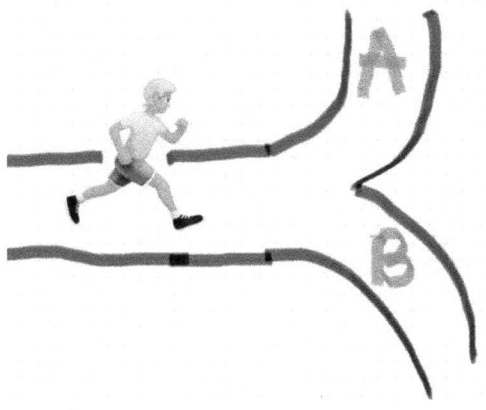

Created with Apple Freeform

Imagine standing at a crossroads; let's call them Path A and B. If you choose Path A, you will win over folks who think that's the right way to go. Those who believe in Path B will disagree and dislike you, if not explicitly, then silently. Meanwhile, there will be a third group that doesn't care what you're doing.

Now, here's where it gets tricky. Let's say you're a people pleaser, desperately looking to win over those who dislike you or are indifferent. Suppose you manage to achieve that. However, by doing so, you risk losing the support of the people behind you. That's because the fact that your supporters were distinct from your detractors from the very start means that your efforts to please those who dislike you and are indifferent may end up antagonizing those who once backed you.

So, in trying to win over everyone, you may find that your original supporters begin to feel alienated, effectively moving to the category of those who now dislike you. The dynamic remains unchanged: no matter how hard you try to gain universal approval, you inevitably sacrifice the support of those who once backed you. Hence, whether you like it or not, you will inevitably experience the 33.33% balance.

The celebrity trap

I know what you're thinking: celebrities, film stars, sports icons, and mass leaders seem to be above the 33.33% rule. After all, figures like Sachin Tendulkar, Amitabh Bachchan, The Rock, and Elon Musk appear universally loved.

But trust me, that's not the case, and it's more of an illusion than reality. The pool of people in these celebrities' lives is exponentially bigger than that of you and me. As a result, the 33.33% of people who genuinely adore them is significantly larger than the total number of people in our lives. That creates the illusion of universal likability, making it seem like they enjoy unwavering support.

While the segment of their admirers may indeed be vast, it doesn't change the fact that there are also critics and detractors for every fan. In reality, the same dynamics of acceptance and rejection exist; it's just that the scale is much more significant in the world of celebrities.

Besides, even gods are not immune to the 33.33% rule, so how can you and I be? Take Hindu gods, for example. Hindus revere them, yet those from other religions often mock them. This pattern holds across all faiths. Every religion has its deities, inspiring devotion among believers while simultaneously drawing criticism from followers of different ideologies.

The risk of bending backwards

When you try to win over every critic or indifferent person, you risk bending over backwards and giving undue importance to those irrelevant to your goals or journey. That often leads to unnecessary stress and depletion of your energy.

Here's an example from my life: while covering foreign exchange markets, I often encountered trolls who disagreed with the views presented in my articles. I vividly remember an email accusing me of manipulating national currencies like the pound and the yen. I chuckled, thinking, "Am I George Soros senior now?" (Trader George Soros is the man who broke the Bank of England's bank by shorting the British Pound.)

In the early days, I responded (perhaps reacted) to every troll, sometimes defensively and engaged in heated banter on social media or via email, trying to debunk their takes and win them over. However, this approach often had the opposite effect. I inadvertently validated random trolls by reacting, diminishing my credibility as a designated analyst.

You can observe this pattern in politics worldwide. The right wing often finds itself desperately trying to win over the left wing, inadvertently elevating the profiles of otherwise struggling film stars, activists, and armchair experts in the process. The same can be said for the left wing when they are in power.

This approach not only creates new "anarchists/social media warriors" but also diverts attention from core issues and the original agendas and ends up weakening core vote banks.

Lesson from Mahabharat

Anger and excessive ego often lead people to commit the same mistake as bending backwards in trying to win over everyone. A powerful example of this can be found in the Kurukshetra war from the Mahabharat.

After the Adharmi Kauravas unfairly killed Arjun's teenage son, Abhimanyu, Arjun vowed publicly to kill Jayadrath before the next day's sunset, declaring that he would immolate himself if he failed. Jaydrath was the one who trapped Abhimanyu inside the defensive "Chakravyuha" formation.

In the heat of the moment, Arjun, the great archer's pride and anger, drove him to make this bold proclamation, inadvertently placing him in a disadvantageous position and bolstering an otherwise relatively easy target Jaydrath's status in the Kaurav army.

The commander of the Kaurav army, Acharya Dron, recognizing Arjun's oath, moved Jayadrath into the innermost area of Chakravyuha, effectively shielding him from Arjun's direct attacks. Consequently, instead of simply eliminating a relatively average combatant, Arjun found himself fighting through a sea of soldiers and obstacles to fulfil his oath.

Arjun's public declaration, driven by ego and anger, wasted time and resources, consuming an entire day of war and delaying the eventual defeat of the Kaurav army.

Arjun could have chosen to remain silent and seek vengeance for his son's death the next day in a matter of minutes. In reality, Jayadrath was petrified at the thought of facing Arjun and contemplated running away from the battlefield that night.

The 33.33% rule applied to human life

The rule can be applied to human life, breaking it down into three key equal parts:

1. Relationships: This sub-sector of life includes all connections, including family, friends, and

romantic partners and represents social support and emotional fulfilment.

2. Work, career, money: The sub-sector covers professional life and everything else that translates into monetary rewards and financial stability.

3. Mental and Physical Health: This dimension focuses on overall well-being, including psychological and physical fitness—a healthy mind in a healthy body.

For most people, one of these sectors thrives at any given time, another may feel lacklustre, and the remaining area remains neutral. For instance, you might find yourself in a fulfilling relationship while career challenges loom and your health feels stable but could be improved. You can have different permutations and combinations.

Some individuals simultaneously excel in all three areas, enjoying a seemingly perfect life. That's rare, but if that's the case, the law of balance states that these individuals have seen all three areas suffer simultaneously in the past and have withered through it, or they might face across-the-board challenges in the future.

This underscores the cyclical nature of life. Maintaining balance among relationships, work, and health is vital as success and struggle coexist.

According to me, the most critical sub-sector of life is health. It's more important than anything else because, ultimately, if you have your health, you can find happiness even if the other two areas – relationships and career – aren't going well. As the saying goes, "Health is wealth."

Imagine having enormous amounts of money and global popularity yet suffering from comorbidities and other significant health issues. Even if the 33.33% representing your relationships and finances are thriving in this scenario, the poor health segment will overshadow everything else.

No matter how successful or well-liked you are, if your health is suffering, you won't be able to fully enjoy the things that are going great in your life.

So, the next time you feel down because a relationship didn't work out or a business deal fell apart, resulting in financial losses, take a moment to draw out the 33.33% rule diagram. Remind yourself that you're still in a good position as long as your health is intact. Solid mental and physical health means you can always bounce back!

4. Understanding Life's Assertions

Mother Nature is a capitalist

A few years ago I watched a gory scene unfold on the National Geographic Channel as a parcel (group of deer) attempted to cross a river. As they navigated the waters, a couple of crocodiles pounced on a few, drowning them while others made it safely to the other side.

The narrator described the whole scene as nature's way of crowding out the weak and leaving only the fittest to survive. Suddenly, a realization struck me that Mother Nature is inherently capitalist.

Mother Nature operates on principles of survival, adaptation, and resource allocation, mirroring capitalist ideals. Darwin's theory of evolution is based on the concept of natural selection. Organisms that adapt to changing environments, compete for basic resources, and exploit available opportunities thrive and reproduce. This survival-focused environment catalyses constant innovation within species, leading to diverse adaptations and behaviours.

For instance, think of cockroaches. It's said that they have survived the asteroid impact that led to the extinction of the mighty dinosaurs 66 million years ago. Their secret to survival is that they can squeeze into tight spaces, allowing them to hide almost anywhere. They are strong, fast, and eat almost everything.

The struggle to survive is akin to businesses vying for market share in the purest form of capitalism where efficiency and adaptability determine success. The entire natural ecosystem reflects capitalist principles, acting like a market force, where the survival of the fittest promotes diversity and resilience within biological groups. The deer that survived did it simply because they were fast, not because they were white or black!

But wait, you might be wondering why the author is discussing this. It's because where I come from, freebies and job quotas are rapidly becoming the "it thing" among politicians and their vote banks.

The trend is concerning as it reflects a growing sentiment that goes against Mother Nature's capitalist tendencies, prioritizing short-term gains over long-term sustainability. While offering freebies may seem like a way to win support and appease voters, it often undermines the necessity for self-reliance, hard work and productivity. It's akin to ensuring the parcel remains weak and falls prey to crocodiles.

Just as nature emphasizes the survival of the fittest, a society that rewards effort and adaptability will likely foster proper growth and prosperity. In contrast, dependency on handouts weakens individuals and communities, much like the weaker deer that don't survive in the wild. That's how politicians create permanent dependencies and vote banks that won't ask tough questions and will vote on handouts.

You might know the tale of a little boy who, trying to be helpful, cut a slit in a cocoon to let a butterfly escape. Sadly, his kind gesture backfired and stunted the butterfly's development. Instead of soaring with strength, the butterfly emerged small, weak, and with crumpled wings—unable to lift off and fly. This tale perfectly illustrates the dangers of tinkering with nature's capitalist put-up or shut-up set-up. It serves as a warning to voters asking for freebies, job quotas, and handouts.

Just as the butterfly needs to struggle to develop healthy wings capable of carrying its weight while flying, individuals require effort and perseverance to grow stronger. So, the only thing voters should expect from politicians is a level playing field and not job quotas, handouts, and freebies.

I fully support helping those weaker sections of society, irrespective of religion, creed, race, and colour, and empowering them to face real-life challenges. For instance, it's always a good idea to lend a hand to students from the weaker sections of society through financial support, books, and study materials. However, when it comes to passing exams and landing a job, candidates must be ready to fight their own battles.

Excellence thrives in any case

This is a must-read section for all those who believe job quotas, freebies, and handouts are empowering. You are probably heading down the wrong path, as true excellence always thrives.

Imagine a hypothetical community, X, that has endured injustice for centuries. Now, X expects politicians to make up for the past by implementing reservations in top universities and the labour market, often overlooking qualifications and exam scores in the process. While the pursuit of equitable opportunities is entirely valid, the route they pursue – reservations – might unintentionally create a cycle of dependency instead of fostering true empowerment.

The thinking is that it will help X compete on equal footing with the so-called privileged class that has successfully cracked the entrance exam, not supposedly through merit, but purportedly due to their perceived advantages and resources.

The belief, however, stems from a misguided notion that top universities are responsible for creating exceptional students when, in reality, the opposite is true. A top university earns its reputation by attracting and gathering excellent students through tough entrance exams. This concentration of talent elevates the university's status and recognition for excellence.

It's a classic example of capitalism, the survival of the fittest at play. When you push students into these prestigious institutions through reservations, you tamper with the filtering process – the entrance exam that demands excellence. This intervention can dilute the university's standards, eroding its appeal relative to other universities.

In time, students who genuinely seek excellence feel compelled to seek out alternative institutions, ultimately leading to the emergence of new top-tier universities.

To summarise, excellence ultimately prevails, just as in economics, where demand and supply always triumph regardless of governmental interventions.

There is no such thing as "struggle"

Human beings are programmed to feel victimized. This tendency spans the spectrum from the rich to the poor and from the successful to those who have faced failures. People have a penchant for portraying themselves as victims, and no other word fuels this feeling as strongly as "struggle."

The dictionary definition of "struggle" is to make violent and strenuous efforts in the face of difficulties or opposition. However, human beings tend to misuse the term to overhype their efforts in achieving their goals as adversity and hardship in a bid to draw sympathy and victim appeal.

Whenever I hear someone proclaiming that they have "struggled a lot," it makes me feel as if they believe their struggles are somehow pivotal to the very fabric of existence of the solar system.

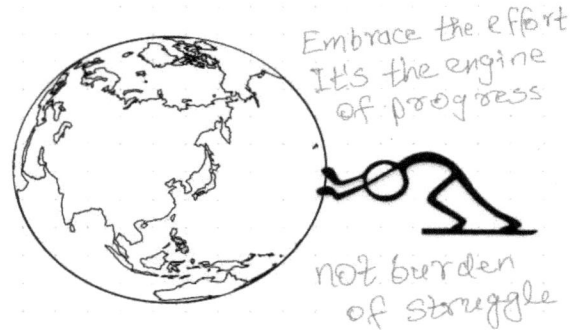

Created with Apple Freeform

And that's the point. There is no such thing as struggle the way it is popularly perceived and marketed. As long as you're aiming to reap the rewards for your efforts, the work you're putting in is fundamentally for your own selfish reasons and doesn't amount to true struggle. You can call it hard work at best.

If you were to work 12 hours a day to earn a salary that benefits an entirely unknown person, you could justify using the word struggle to describe your life. But let's keep in perspective that even today, in some parts of the world, individuals work for pennies in hazardous conditions, enduring grueling conditions for mere survival.

If you are physically fit and not toiling in hazardous environments, you're likely in a much better position than you might think. Establishing a cottage industry around your supposed struggles in life is unnecessary.

Instead of fixating on minor difficulties, it's crucial to recognize your advantages and the opportunities available to you instead of exaggerating hardships to gain sympathy or recognition.

Avoid the vicious cycle

Note that being addicted to the concept of "struggle" is the first step in setting off a chain reaction that can ultimately lead you to the depths of a victim mentality. Once you start believing that you have struggled significantly, a sense of entitlement can quickly take root.

This entitlement often breeds jealousy toward those who possess what you desire. Instead of focusing on your path and effort, you may begin to resent others for their successes. This mindset can lead to a push for activism that advocates for freebies and handouts as you start to feel that you deserve support without the corresponding effort or merit.

Ultimately, this cycle can culminate in a shift toward victimhood and, even more troubling, mental depression.

The key to avoiding this is to forget the concept of struggle as it is popularly understood. As Shri Krishna said in Bhagwad Geeta, life itself is not possible without action, or "karma." This encompasses every aspect of existence, even our choices about doing nothing.

In essence, choosing inaction is also a form of action. So, suppose you are going to be in action anyway. Why not choose to diligently work toward your aspirations rather than be a crybaby and fall into the trap of perceiving our efforts as mere "struggles" and victimhood?

There is no such thing as an "optimum or ideal life"

The search for an optimum or ideal life is one of the biggest sources of frustration today. The pursuit of this high standard leads to immense pressure and dissatisfaction. But, take it from me that no such thing as an optimum life truly exists, and I will illustrate this point with concepts from economics.

Keynesian economists often discuss the concept of optimum capacity utilization. This term refers to the level at which factors of production, be it labour, machinery, or capital, are being used most effectively to maximize output without causing strain on the system. You may have seen business leaders talk about capacity utilization and how optimum levels can be reached with lower borrowing costs (I have yet to meet a business person who says interest rates are ideal and don't need to go lower ☺).

The idea of optimum capacity utilization, however, is flawed in some respects because capacity utilization is essentially an engineering concept. For instance, imagine a classroom with 10 benches accommodating two students each. In this case, the optimum capacity utilization is defined as 21 people, comprising 20 students and one teacher.

Now, consider a scenario where you open a coaching centre for engineering students with a capacity of 21 people in a location dominated by a commerce college. Given this context, your classroom is rarely full. That might lead to the conclusion that there is no optimum capacity utilization. Theoretically, that could seem accurate, but practically, it tells a different story.

The fact is that at any given point when considering specific circumstances and demand-supply dynamics, whatever is happening is always optimum. The fact that students are enrolling in the first year, despite the location disadvantages, indicates optimum capacity utilization. So, achieving "optimum" is not strictly about filling every available seat; it's about getting the hang of context and dynamics to play.

Translating this observation to life, as resources in an economy cannot always be perfectly optimized, our lives cannot follow a singular model of success or happiness. In other words, with a given level of effort and uncontrollable macro factors, whatever happens in your life is always optimal at any given time.

When people talk about achieving optimum conditions, they often unknowingly yearn for a specific set of circumstances that will yield the desired outcome. In other words, the concept of "optimum" is not static; it constantly evolves as the factors we can control, along with those beyond our control, change over time. This shifting landscape means that what might be considered optimal today could be different tomorrow due to new circumstances, emerging information, or unexpected challenges.

Viewing life through this lens means you will always remain aware that your concept of "optimum" is truly a specific combination of controllable and uncontrollable factors. By recognizing this, you'll focus your energy on taking actionable steps to ensure that the aspects you can control are being effectively managed.

This proactive mindset encourages you to concentrate on the things within your power – such as your efforts, attitude, decision-making, and preparation – rather than relying on luck to come through or shifting the blame for failures onto circumstances beyond your control.

Returning to the classroom example, if you want your classroom to be full, you must consider various actionable steps, such as relocating closer to an engineering college and investing more in advertising your program to attract more students. Additionally, hiring professors with strong track records and reputations can boost the quality of education you offer, bringing more students.

All this means taking charge of the factors that you can control. It's important to remember that you can only rightfully complain about luck or circumstances beyond your control when you are 100% sure that you have already mastered everything within your influence.

Henceforth, before attributing your setbacks to external forces, revisit this analogy of optimum capacity utilization and evaluate whether you have done everything in your power to achieve the so-called optimum.

The desired result isn't guaranteed

Constant connectivity, information overload, and influencer culture have contributed to Gen Z developing a "control freak" mentality. They often feel the need to control every aspect of their lives and expect flawless results every time, believing that the outcome is directly tied to their input.

This belief is further reinforced in schools and colleges, where the link between effort and outcome is clear: if you thoroughly study the assigned material, a top rank is guaranteed. Therefore, students come to expect that their efforts will always translate into success. The equation seems simple—study hard, achieve high marks—but the reality is often more complicated.

I'm not saying that output isn't influenced by input; of course, it is. That said, there are numerous factors that can't be controlled but can single-handedly make or break the expected outcome.

Let's take the example of Mr Alex, a top performer at a leading IT firm. He has been dedicated to completing projects, putting in maximum effort, and steering clear of office politics – all of which ideally set him up for a favorable year-end appraisal and promotion.

However, by the end of the year, the IT sector slips into a recession, creating a challenging environment for heavily indebted firms like the one Alex works for. Despite his outstanding performance, Alex faces disappointment: he won't receive the appraisal and promotion he should have earned. (Or the fact that he hasn't been laid off in a recession is perhaps an appraisal. But it takes a little bit of grey hair to realize that). What happened here? A macro force, clearly beyond Alex's control, has derailed his prospects. This situation serves as a potent reminder that, no matter how hard we work, external circumstances can impact the outcomes of our efforts.

In such scenarios, it's essential for Alex and all of us to accept these realities as part of life.

The takeaway is that there are uncontrollable factors in every aspect of life. Accepting such factors is pivotal in ensuring our mental and physical well-being while we chase our dreams. It's in these areas, where our control ends, the idea of God comes into play.

When Shri Krishna stated that Arjuna is the greatest archer of all time, he talked about Arjuna's exceptional ability to control the bow and arrow before it's released. His skill and precision in aiming and firing are unparalleled. However, once the arrow is in flight, Arjuna has no control over its trajectory or whether it will hit the desired target.

Several external factors can play spoilsport, keeping the end goal out of our reach. For instance, a sudden change in weather conditions, gusts of wind, or an equally agile target can all lead to Arjuna's arrow missing its mark. That's despite Arjuna being the greatest archer of all time. It's a powerful metaphor for life itself. While we can control our actions and efforts, like Arjuna skilfully drawing back his bow, once we set our intentions in motion, countless variables beyond our influence can affect the outcome.

That's also why we should remain humble in our victories and not be deterred by our failures. In both scenarios, external factors beyond our control play a significant role.

There is no such thing as "retirement"

Featuring high on the list of what makes an ideal or optimum life for people worldwide is that damn thing called "retirement." Yes, I dislike that manufactured illusion of "Ohh, I have done my part in life and will now rest on my laurels, preaching wisdom to one and all."

Retirement, as we know, is a relatively new invention, not a natural stage of life but a socially constructed idea that has been drilled into our consciousness such that now it feels like it's a natural stage of life. The narrative is so pervasive that 4-5 -year- old kids, who can barely speak two logical sentences, understand it: grandparents retire, stop working, and "rest and enjoy their remaining life." The narrative has been sold to us as the ultimate reward for decades of hard work, but it's actually a trap.

It all started in 1881 when the conservative German chancellor, Otto Von Bismarck, launched a strategic manoeuvre against Marxists by announcing that anyone over70 would be forced to retire in exchange for a pension. This ground breaking policy was one of the first instances of a social safety net designed to provide financial support to the elderly, establishing a precedent that would eventually evolve into modern pension systems.

Today, this initial idea has transformed into a global phenomenon of epic proportions. Pension-related issues now possess the power to make or break governments in democratic nations.

But it's a trap that leads to adverse mental conditioning:

Premature Aging: The constant messaging about eventually "winding down" and "taking it easy" leads us to associate aging with physical and mental weakness. This creates self-limiting beliefs, ensuring that we never realize our full potential.

It's akin to a bullock cart where the cart pushes the horse forward; we set ourselves up for self-termination or deterioration due to an ingrained belief in the concept of retirement. In reality, we should retire only when our bodies signal that it's time to do so.

An analogy from my own life illustrates this well. Now nearing 40, I continue to lift weights – a passion I embraced at 16. I still engage in intense, high-intensity workouts just as I did in my teens and twenties, often feeling sore a day after.

The difference now is that every time I end up sore, my wife and mom both urge me to consider my age and reduce the intensity of my training programs (the cart pushing the horse). My response is always the same: let my body dictate the intensity of my workouts. If my body tells me to slow down, then I will even if I don't want to. This attitude has helped me not only delay aging but also maintain my fitness, while many of my friends have succumbed to the age narrative and developed self-inflicted weaknesses.

Remember, if you don't use it, you lose it and retirement makes sure you don't use it.

Dependency: Sure pension helps and provides much-needed support, but the reality is that it often fails to keep pace with inflation. This asks for a question: does your pension truly offer financial security in the long run?

Moreover, relying on a pension effectively places you at the mercy of politicians and their policies. It's not a surprise that many retirees become single-issue voters, prioritizing parties that promise to care for their financial needs above all else. For them, concerns about pensions overshadow other important issues, often putting them at odds with what the working population desires from the government. That's a net negative for the nation in the long run.

Horrible economics: Life expectancy has dramatically increased worldwide over the last century, leading to growing concerns about the fiscal sustainability of pension systems.

Retirees, through their steady spending financed by pensions and savings, contribute to inflation in the economy without adding to productivity. While it's true that they significantly contributed to GDP and productivity during their working years, that value has already been accounted for.

Now, as they draw from these pensions and savings, retirees are often consuming resources without participating in the creation of new value. This dynamic poses a significant economic challenge, as the influx of pension-funded spending can exacerbate inflation while simultaneously straining the systems designed to support them.

It's still the jungle law out there

Let's revisit the example of the deer crossing crocodile-infested waters. Do crocodiles spare old deer? Not at all. In the wild, survival is dictated by harsh realities, where the strong prevail, and the weak face significant peril. This illustrates that anything that weakens us, including the notion of retirement, should be reconsidered. As harsh or heartless as it may sound, that's the plain truth. However, it's important to recognize that human beings have evolved to be more humane, kind, and considerate toward both the young and the old.

I wholeheartedly support taking care of those who are genuinely weak and in need of assistance. But when it comes to those who are fit and healthy, choosing to retire simply because they've reached a self-imposed age threshold doesn't seem right.

History bears witness to this perspective. Over the centuries, we have seen remarkable warriors over the age of 60 achieve extraordinary feats of strength and skill on the battlefield, achievements that many 20-year-olds today might find difficult to replicate.

A prime example is Kondaji Ramji Shelar, a commander in the army of the 17th century Maratha Empire under Chhatrapati Shivaji Maharaj. Alongside his niece Tanaji Rao Malusare, the Chief Commander in the Battle of Sinhagad, and Sardar Suryaji Malusare, Kondaji scaled the treacherous Sinhagad Fort using only a rope in complete darkness. In a remarkable display of courage and skill, Kondaji, at the age of 80, yes, you read that correctly, defeated Mughal commander Udaybhan Rathod with his sword in a gripping battle of nerves.

I am sure there are many such examples in world history.

So, how did they do it at the age of 60 or more? The straightforward answer is they never had any idea of this thing called "retirement". These warriors embraced a lifestyle of continuous engagement and activity.

I have moved beyond the concept of retirement and plan to continue working right up to my last day on this planet and you should too. I believe in the value of staying active, engaged, and contributing – both personally and professionally – regardless of age. Moreover, I'm committed to ensuring that my kids don't internalize the notion of retirement either.

Post-retirement plans are true passions

It is said that the best career lies in following your passion... that is one thing you can dedicate long hours to and still feel energized simply because you love doing it.

One of the simplest ways to uncover this passion is by listing the activities you envision pursuing after retirement. Those pursuits often represent your true love and passion.

The activities we want to engage in after retirement are driven by genuine enjoyment and enthusiasm, rather than external pressures like financial gain or career advancement. Thus, jotting down post-retirement plans is a great way of exploring your genuine interests, revealing what you genuinely care about and want to invest your time in.

One might consider pursuing those post-retirement plans from the 30s, if not full-time, then part-time. That could lead to a more fulfilling and balanced career journey throughout your life.

I know what you're thinking: the passion I discovered won't make big money. After all, making money is equally important when we're young, and I agree completely.

Again, remember that you can pursue a passion part-time if a full-time engagement isn't possible or financially feasible. And who knows, your part-time passion could eventually generate more income than you initially anticipated.

By balancing your financial responsibilities and interests, you create an opportunity to explore your passions without sacrificing stability, potentially leading to unexpected rewards along the way. Embrace the journey and keep an open mind; you never know where it might lead!

Gig economy for you

Note that following your passions and remaining active in a financially rewarding way throughout your life has never been easier, thanks to the gig economy. Recently an old interview of LinkedIn co-founder Reid Hoffman has gone viral on social media in which he predicts that by 2034, the 9 to 5 job will be replaced by a gig economy – a contract with multiple companies and work across various industries. A recent article by The Economic Times described the gig economy as "Specialized skills + global demand = premium rates."

The setup encourages individuals to leverage their expertise and experience in innovative ways, providing opportunities for continuous learning and earning.

5. Mindset And Perspective

You and your problems are not special

Recently, I watched a web series titled Kota Factory, which delves into the lives of students preparing for the IIT entrance exam, one of the toughest in the world. The main character (student) faces difficulties concentrating on his studies, struggles with loss of appetite, experiences sleepless nights, and feels overwhelmed by stress while living in a hostel away from his family.

After hearing the issue, the teacher calmly responds that these problems are nothing new, emphasizing a crucial point: first, we must rid ourselves of the notion that every child is special. That is a myth. In truth, no one is inherently special; everyone is born the same, and the challenges we face are common experiences shared by many.

Hearing this struck a chord with me. Bingo! That's the secret to overcoming most issues: stop treating yourself and your problems as special, and challenge the popular sentiment that says so. (after all, the crowd is always wrong!)

Humans, especially in the modern era, are often programmed to feel victimized. The problem begins when one starts to consider themselves as special. Once you adopt this mindset, every problem begins to feel unique and overwhelming. Because it feels special, you may also believe there is no viable solution; it becomes easy to attribute your struggles to luck, the stars, or perceived favoritism from a higher power.

The above line of thinking can lead to a sense of helplessness, where challenges seem insurmountable, and you fall into the trap of blaming external forces for conspiring against you.

At its core, this perception stems from overthinking, a feature of human beings. Nature has endowed us with remarkable intelligence that enables us to go beyond mere existence and assess and interpret every situation and development. However, this gift is a double-edged sword.

While our capacity for critical thinking and analysis has propelled our progress, it is also the root cause of overthinking, where we become entangled in a web of thoughts and assumptions.

Animals don't face this issue because they are not blessed with advanced cognitive function. Have you ever seen a street dog stop barking and sulk in a corner after someone screamed and threw stones at it? Unlike humans, who might overthink and internalize these experiences, the dog's reaction is instinctual. It will run away and seek safety but never give up barking. It's the same for all animals except humans. We overthink, which leads us to doubt our abilities and second-guess our choices, causing us to give up meaningful or beneficial pursuits.

Recognizing that you and your problems are not unique helps avoid overthinking and regain control of the situation. By letting go of the idea that you're special in your struggles, you open yourself up to the shared experiences of humanity and the potential solutions that come from resilience and persistence.

Created with Apple Freeform

Remember that humans have existed on this planet for approximately six million years. It means that somewhere in the vast span of human history, someone has undoubtedly encountered and overcome the challenges you are facing, be it related to finance, health, family, romance or other things.

This realization is incredibly liberating and, at the same time, empowering in taking control of our lives.

And if that doesn't convince you, consider this: each and every one of us will eventually exit the earth and be forgotten entirely. Some achievers may be remembered for a few decades, others for centuries, and a rare few for a couple of thousand years, but ultimately, they too will fade into obscurity. That's an undeniable fact.

Ever wonder how many civilizations have thrived and vanished right beneath the very spot where you're sitting and reading this? It's quite likely that the place where you live has a history of cultures that have risen and fallen, their stories lost to time, just like we will be. This perspective reinforces the idea that, on a macro level, the universe can seem devoid of inherent meaning.

Given this reality, there's no merit in treating ourselves or our problems as uniquely special. Understanding our place in the grand scheme of things can be humbling and liberating.

Embracing tunnel vision

"In the long run, we are all dead," British economist John Maynard Keynes once said. I will say the same about life to remind you that while it's natural to plan for the future, we must not neglect the significance of the present or living the moment.

Our ability to overthink often causes us to fixate too much on the long run or the end product, leading us to overlook the importance of being present in the moment and efficiently executing the tasks at hand. In other words, focusing too much on the future or the end product often leads to losing focus on what it takes to get there.

So, the key to success and mental well-being lies in adopting tunnel vision – staying squarely focused on "one step, one punch, one round at a time," as Rocky advises Apollo's son in the movie Creed.

Consider this example: imagine you're planning to drive 200 miles from point A to point B for some work today. Even though you're familiar with the route, would you really stand on top of your car to check the road conditions 10 or 20 miles ahead of where you are? That would be impossible! Even if Google Maps indicates traffic jams 10 miles ahead, you still start your journey focusing on the next 100 meters as they come. All the while, you hope for a smooth ride ahead.

As you continue your journey and encounter obstacles along the way in the form of bad roads and traffic, you adjust your route, divert when necessary, and take whatever actions are needed to continue your journey. In some cases, you might even decide to abandon or postpone the trip.

The analogy tells us that being flexible and living the moment allows you to navigate life's complexities while maintaining your focus on the present, ultimately leading you to your destination successfully.

Remember that your ability to focus on the "now" is closely linked to how much you enjoy the journey compared to the outcome. If you're overly focused on the end result, the process can feel challenging or tedious, making it hard to live in the moment.

Take Mr. A, for instance. He's obsessed with developing six-pack abs solely to impress girls. However, he's so fixated on that goal that he lacks genuine interest in the process itself. Because of this, he'll likely struggle to maintain the tunnel vision needed to enjoy his workouts and reach his destination.

On the other hand, there's Mr. B, who loves to sweat it out each day. Because he genuinely enjoys the process, there's a strong chance he'll end up with the six-pack that Mr. A covets.

Broken window fallacy of life and drama triangle

One of the most common clichés is the idea of being helpful to everyone, even when assistance isn't requested, with the belief that it will spark a ripple effect of kindness and create what I like to call a "pyramid of happiness."

In fact, there's a Bollywood movie where the protagonist espouses the idea that if you help three people, they'll help three more, setting off a chain reaction that leads to a joyful society.

As appealing as this vision may seem, it ultimately paves the way for the "Drama Triangle," a dynamic that cultivates victimhood and triggers exhausting emotional swings as individuals fluctuate between the roles of victim, rescuer, and persecutor.

A fitting analogy from economics is the "broken window/glass fallacy." Assume a severe recession has hit the global economy, causing your close friend, who repairs windows and glass, to lose his business. To help him, you devise a seemingly brilliant idea: break the excellent window glass in your living room so your friend can repair it for a fee. The thinking is that the friend, motivated by the money earned, will spend at least a part of it elsewhere, helping someone else earn an income, who will spend money elsewhere. The process will set off a virtuous cycle of consumption, spending, investment, and economic growth, ultimately stabilizing the global economy.

As appealing as it sounds, the whole process is flawed because the initial transaction is fundamentally flawed. By breaking your excellent window, you wasted money that could have been used productively for a more meaningful benefit, yielding a longer-lasting positive multiplier effect on the economy.

The example mirrors the idea of being overly available to help everyone create a positive change in society. Just as breaking the window doesn't contribute to any actual economic improvement, unrequested help doesn't make the world a better place. (This is another example of why crowd and popular sentiment is always wrong!)

It often triggers an emotional reaction where we believe that if we help someone, they will feel obligated to help us in return. This dynamic sets off a cycle of unfulfilled expectations and disappointment, as opposed to the genuine connections we seek to foster and it inadvertently traps us in the role of "victim" within the Drama Triangle.

The Drama Triangle, first proposed by San Francisco psychiatrist Stephen B. Karpman in 1968, is a model that illustrates a dysfunctional social interaction where individuals assume one of three roles: Victim, Rescuer, and Persecutor.

In the example above, we position ourselves as the victim because we helped someone but have yet to receive any assistance in return. The individual who hasn't reciprocated becomes the persecutor. At the same time, a third party, referred to as the rescuer, may step in, voluntarily supporting our case and seeking to address the supposed injustice.

Human beings love to portray themselves as victims, and hence, most of us are trapped in the triangle in some or other aspect of life. I am sure you have come across people who are always available to help and then sulk in isolation, celebrating victimhood. It's too addictive! After all, being a victim helps us garner attention and sympathy and seek favours that otherwise might not come through.

However, it comes at an expense. The mental and emotional strain of playing the victim accrues over time, reducing productivity and causing tangible and intangible damage.

Exercise

> ➢ List specific instances where you went out of your way to help someone (I am not talking about helping an old person cross the road) without being asked.

> ➢ Did you anticipate receiving something in return for your assistance?

> Did the reciprocation come through quickly, or did you find yourself waiting a long time? During that wait, did you feel angry or frustrated with the person who was supposed to return the favour?

> Did you end up as a victim in the drama triangle?

Sunk cost fallacy

A sunk cost is an expense that has already been incurred and is non-recoverable. We often cling to unworthy paths because of these sunk costs.

Here is an example. A distant relative of mine enrolled his daughter in an engineering college because her older cousin had pursued engineering and landed a high-paying job, placing her in India's top income tax bracket.

The problem, however, was that my relative's daughter wasn't suited for engineering, and it quickly became evident as she started accumulating backlogs (KTs). Ideally, she would have transitioned to commerce or another field that aligned better with her strengths.

Yet, they insisted on sticking with the engineering path. Why? Because they had already invested a significant amount of money into engineering, changing streams now would feel like admitting a loss. This kind of thinking is fundamentally flawed. Decisions can often go awry and should be reassessed.

Continuing down this route simply because of the money already spent reflects short-sighted reasoning. The sunk cost-led rigid attitude means that in the long run, the distant relatives' daughter will not reach her true potential and will likely face increased frustration, unhappiness, and financial instability.

This scenario is a classic example of the sunk cost fallacy, where individuals are trapped by their past investments instead of making rational decisions based on future possibilities.

I won't go into more details and say just this: Move over sunk costs!

The "listen to your heart" bullshit

I'm sure you've noticed how film stars, business tycoons, and successful individuals often claim they succeeded by following their "heart" or "mind"–that supposed impulsive inner voice representing pure desires, untainted by materialism and intensely spiritual.

In India, this has become a scam. Celebrities consistently echo the same sentiment, and in my opinion, it's a facade for television – a line that sounds good and sells tickets. The idea that they followed their inner voice resonates with audiences, giving off an aura of authenticity and inspiration. After all, how would you feel if a film star or business tycoon says I pursued this idea because there was money to be made!

The brutal honesty is a turn-off for most. But the reality is precisely that. Most of these successful figures are cold and calculating, weighing their decisions based on careful assessments of risk and monetary reward. In other words, they trust their brains, the rational voice that provides logical answers... always and in all situations.

Do you remember that girl who always seemed out of your league? Your brain probably recognized this from day one, reminding you of the reality of the situation. Yet, your heart and emotions took over, urging you to pursue her. I will remind you of what happened next – You were friend-zoned, where your feelings weren't reciprocated as you hoped, and you probably ended up attending her marriage.

Consider another example. Criminals know their actions are wrong; their brains warn them against it, yet they still commit the crime because they follow their impulses rather than their rational instincts. More often than not, they seek intoxication before committing the crime. That helps silence the rational voice, allowing impulses and desires to take over, leading to misguided decisions.

Mind or heart is always irrational, and allowing it to dominate the rational brain is an open invitation to disaster. Astrology considers the moon, the planet representing the mind/desires, a malefic entity that can lead you to disaster.

The best way to avoid finding yourself in situations like that is to take a moment to write things down and reflect on them during a 15- to 20-minute walk. This practice allows you to clear your mind and gain perspective. As you physically move and breathe, you create space for your thoughts to settle, enabling brain dominance over the heart.

The misleading dropout by choice narrative

Let's dive into dopamine-boosting narratives that resonate with Gen Z, and one that's particularly striking is the "dropout by choice" thing.

For that, I blame Bill Gates, the legendary founder of Microsoft and one of the wealthiest people on the planet. Well, it's not really his fault, but the problem is how his story is misinterpreted and put forward to youngsters worldwide.

Gates famously dropped out of the prestigious Harvard University halfway through to start Microsoft, and the rest, as they say, is history. Gates' story is thrown around as a source of inspiration everywhere. But honestly, the story is consumed in a wrong way.

Here's the thing: people everywhere seem to think that dropping out of college is a sign of genius. But let's be honest: Gates dropped out of Harvard, not some local college that doesn't even make it into the top 1,000 institutions in the country. Take a moment to consider that. Getting accepted to such a prestigious school alone signifies excellence and serious potential. (How many of you can even think of dropping out of Harvard, assuming you are admitted to the university?)

Meanwhile, everyday folks like me hear Gates' story and believe we can drop out of college just as Gates did and somehow replicate his success. That kind of thinking is out there! Ask yourself: how many people drop out of Harvard every year to pursue Microsoft-like ventures? How many Bill Gates are out there today, claiming to have dropped out of a prestigious university by choice to create a billion-dollar empire? What's the actual percentage of successful individuals who are top college dropouts?

The answer to these questions is a big fat negligible! Life is all about averages and probabilities. Most successful people have a strong academic background and so should you, if you desire success.

Don't get me wrong; I'm not saying you should squash your entrepreneurial spirit If you have a brilliant idea, definitely pursue it! Just remember that dropping out because you think you'll magically become a success like Gates is nothing more than a dopamine trap. Sure, if you have a great idea, go for it! But do it thoughtfully after considering all the angles and possibilities.

6. Acceptance And Growth

Accepting limitations

Think about how a smartphone is designed with specific features. Some models emphasize camera quality, while others prioritize battery life or processing speed. Each model has limitations in some areas, but those limitations are what make it specialized. Users choose their devices based on their own needs and preferences.

Similar to smartphones, we all have our features and limitations. While many of us readily embrace our strengths, we often shy away from acknowledging our weaknesses, particularly those that are inherent. Accepting that some drawbacks are inherent, part of our DNA can be empowering. These innate traits might include aspects of our personality, specific physical attributes, or even predispositions to particular challenges.

For instance, if you tend to be impulsive, you may have inherited this characteristic from your parents. It is an intrinsic issue that may never disappear entirely.

Now, imagine this impulsivity as a large stone blocking your path on a road. You can't simply pick it up and throw it aside, so what do you do? You learn to negotiate with the situation. You either find a way around it, or climb over it to move ahead.

Similarly, instead of obsessing over eliminating your inherent impulsiveness, you can develop strategies to navigate around it. These might include practicing mindfulness, counting to ten, setting similar guidelines to avoid jumping the gun, and seeking ways to channel the inherent weakness into positive action. By doing so, you continue to move forward while being comfortable with your inherent weakness.

The perfect example of an individual bypassing his inherent weakness to succeed is Thomas Edison, an American inventor and businessman, whose contributions to the field of electric power generation, mass communication, sound recording, and motion pictures have left a long- lasting impact on humanity. Edison, known for his remarkable inventiveness and determination, faced significant challenges throughout his life. One of his inherent drawbacks was his academic struggle; he was labelled as a slow learner and had difficulty in traditional schooling. That could have been the "big stone" of his life, blocking his path to success.

Instead of trying to remove that stone or letting it defeat him, he chose to negotiate with his situation. He took an unconventional route to learning, often conducting experiments and engaging with practical work rather than adhering strictly to classroom teachings. It is said that his mother home- schooled him to accommodate his learning style, allowing him to thrive in a hands-on environment.

Edison didn't let his academic challenges stop him; instead, he found ways to climb over that stone by focusing on his strengths in experimentation and innovation. His ability to see challenges as opportunities for learning led him to become one of the greatest inventors in history, with over a thousand patents to his name.

This example shows how getting comfortable with inherent traits or limitations, rather than trying to eliminate or deny them, can lead to remarkable achievements. Like finding a way around or over a stone in your path, Edison devised ways that allowed him to navigate his challenges and succeed.

The survival mechanism kicks in as we accept mistakes

It was 2011, my first year trading commodities, and on one Friday morning, I took a short position in crude oil that would have profited from an expected price drop in what is popularly known as black gold. My decision to short oil, whose price is closely tied to global economic health, was driven by a bearish technical setup and other macro factors, and prices began to decline immediately.

However, later in the day, the U.S. monthly jobs report hit the wires, blowing past expectations to signal a red-hot labour market and strength in the world's largest economy. And so, oil prices reversed their losses and climbed higher for the day. Ideally, I should have reassessed the situation closed the short position in light of such a strong jobs report and switched to a bullish long position heading into the weekend.

But, my ego came in between me and my rational brain and I struggled to accept that my initial analysis was now wrong. Instead of pivoting, I held onto my short position, hoping that prices would eventually fall back. My emotional attachment to the trade overpowered my rational judgment, and I spent the entire weekend feeling anxious, unable to sleep, and desperately seeking information that would support my bearish bias – a classic example of human behaviour.

My frustration and mental fog increased multi-fold on Monday as oil prices rose further, cheering the strong U.S. labour market. I struggled to think rationally. Eventually, the pain of holding the loss-making position became unbearable, and I threw in the towel. I closed my shorts and exited the market.

But then, something remarkable happened – the fog of pain and frustration immediately lifted, and my rational brain kicked in, giving me a clear perspective on the situation. I immediately assessed that the strength of the U.S. economy meant oil could continue to rise, so I decided to go long, and by the next day, I made a profit that allowed me to recover my losses.

After exiting the short position, my ego took a backseat to rational decision-making. That's a vital lesson in life and trading.

The key takeaway is accepting mistakes is genuinely empowering. Our brains are hardwired for survival, and once we accept our mistakes, this survival mechanism activates, ensuring we think clearly and make rational decisions.

Various studies have demonstrated that accepting and reflecting on mistakes lead to improved cognitive flexibility. For instance, research on "psychological acceptance" shows that people who acknowledge their mistakes are better equipped to adapt and find solutions, dedicating energy to productive actions rather than wrestling with overthinking, regret, and shame.

In her work "Dare to Lead," Brown discusses the importance of vulnerability, including accepting mistakes, as key to courage and effective leadership. Accepting mistakes creates an environment where individuals feel safe to learn, innovate, and take risks.

In "The Power of Now," Eckhart Tolle says that embracing mistakes without judgment allows individuals to release negative thoughts and emotions, freeing mental energy for more constructive thinking and planning.

Mistake Reflection Exercise

Make a list of all mistakes/wrongdoing over the past 12 months. After that,

- Briefly describe each mistake.
- How long did it take you to come to terms with them?
- Mood Changes: How did your mood change during this time?
- After Acceptance: How did your mood shift after you accepted the mistake?
- Assess what stopped you from coming to terms with the mistake in the first place.

Understanding luck and skill

In a world where some seem to catch a lucky break while others constantly face hurdles, it's common for people programmed for victimhood to lament their misfortune.

"If only I had better luck!" they exclaim, blaming their setbacks on an absence of serendipity. While luck can play a role in our lives, fixating solely on it can close our eyes to an important truth: Luck is useless without skills.

Imagine you are at a bar with friends, enjoying your Friday evening beer, and the discussion turns to setbacks and failures. One friend discusses her failed startup, blaming it on bad luck. Another friend expresses frustration from being overlooked for a promotion, casually brushing it off as just a matter of being in the wrong place at the wrong time. Meanwhile, someone in the corner quietly listens, nodding, perhaps thinking about walking the fine line between skill and luck.

This scenario captures a common mindset, worrying about luck while overlooking the importance of building skills that can shape our future.

Think of it like having access to leverage in a trading account: your broker might offer you 100% leverage, allowing you to buy stocks worth much more than the total amount of money you've got in your account. But if you don't understand trading, that leverage won't lead you anywhere good.

Now, contrast that with someone who has taken the time to learn the ropes, digging into market trends, taking courses, and perfecting their strategies. They can make several times more money than you with little to no leverage.

In other words, what matters is not how lucky someone is but how skilled they are at leveraging that luck when it starts to shine. It's all about being prepared and ready to take action when the Sun shines and turn fortunate opportunities into meaningful success.

The point is, while it's tempting to blame luck for our struggles, doing so distracts us from the real deal: to make the most of any fortunate turn, we need to equip ourselves with the skills and knowledge to seize those opportunities.

Now you might think: Is there a secret to success, mastering a skill, and determining when luck might shine? There is, read the next topic.

7. Practical Guidance

The Key to success is "repetitive 'submaximal' effort"

Now that you understand the importance of being skilled rather than being lucky, you may be eager to know about that secret strategy to excel in any skills you wish to pursue so that you are ready to shine when the luck shines.

Well, I'm here to tell you that there's no secret sauce when it comes to success; it stems from straightforward, repetitive, submaximal effort. And I will illustrate this with an example that will resonate with everyone: the process of learning how to write... remember we all went through this in our early life and excelled in it.

Learning to write involves hand-eye coordination, fine motor skills, and cognitive processes. Several scientific studies have examined how children develop these skills during handwriting practice. The findings indicated that writing requires fine motor control and an understanding of spatial relationships between letters and words on a page.

It's one of the world's most challenging exercises or skill development programs. Don't just take my word for it – try writing with your non-dominant hand. Promise yourself that you will write one page daily with your weaker hand, and I can almost guarantee that you'll give up after just a few days.

That's because the challenge of coordinating movements, forming letters, and maintaining legibility is no small feat!

Still, we all have mastered the skill of writing, and how did we achieve this? It was through repeated submaximal effort coupled with progressive overload. Around age four, **we began with short daily** writing sessions or dictation exercises that typically lasted five to ten minutes, a submaximal effort. Imagine if your first day of school involved an hour-long writing exercise. You would never want to return to school again. So, the key here is consistent "submaximal" effort.

The initial effort helped develop essential motor skills and letter recognition ability in a manageable and stress-free environment.

As we grew older, our writing practice gradually broadened. By the time we reached the age of 8 or 9, those short sessions turned into more intensive writing tasks of composing descriptive essays and completing three/four hours-long examination papers. This progression wasn't sudden; it was a slow and steady process of natural evolution fuelled by consistent practice and increasing complexity in the tasks we undertook.

Just as athletes build strength by gradually increasing the weights they lift, we, too, enhance our writing abilities by confronting slightly greater challenges each time.

Repeated, consistent submaximal effort plays a crucial role in helping the brain develop new neural pathways. Engaging in tasks that challenge us without overwhelming our capacities promotes brain plasticity or the brain's ability to adapt and reorganize to new learning, experiences, and stress. When we repeatedly practice a skill or activity at a manageable intensity, it reinforces existing connections in the brain while forming new ones.

Consider the example of construction workers and wage laborers. I've noticed that many over 50 are often fitter and stronger than the average 20-year-old from well-to-do families who lift heavy weights and train one body part each day for muscle failure.

These workers participate in physically demanding tasks with submaximal workloads that engage their entire bodies day in and day out. This consistent level of activity spurs strength and endurance gains over the years. Unlike ego-lifters and weekend warriors, who lift excessively heavy weights to end up sore and undergo long recovery periods, these workers rely on their regular routines that involve manageable loads. Their consistent submaximal stress allows their bodies to adapt to the stress enabling them to build and maintain strength and fitness well into old age.

That's all there is to it! The route to success in any field follows this same fundamental process.

If something seems to work in the blink of an eye, it's likely a trap or a mirage that won't provide lasting results. Quick fixes and instant gratification can be tempting but often lead to disappointment and superficial outcomes.

Tracking Saturn for expectations management

You might call astrology hocus pocus or pseudo-science, but if looked at logically while bypassing the religious shenanigans, it helps practically manage expectations, a key to being happy.

I like to keep a close eye on Saturn's transits.

Saturn takes roughly 30 years to transit through the 12 houses of the zodiac. Transit from the 12th to the 8th houses from the moon is a period where it's essential to keep your expectations grounded and focus on hard work, honing your skills in preparation for the opportunities that come with the subsequent transits.

This is the time to follow Shri Krishna's advice from Bhagavad Gita Chapter 2: कर्मण्येवाधिकारस्ते मा फलेषु कदाचन। मा कर्मफलहेतुर्भूर्मा ते सङ्गोऽस्त्वकर्मणि, which means -You have the right to work only but never to its fruits. Let not the fruits of action be your motive, nor let your attachment be to inaction.

Later, you'll want to gear up for the 7.5-year lucky period during the transits through the 9th, 10th, and 11th houses. During these times, the groundwork you've laid can begin to pay off, and you may find that your efforts align with favourable outcomes.

During these years, you will find that life provides you with greater leverage in your personal "trading account," allowing you to maximize opportunities based on the skill set you've developed during the preceding transit from the 12th house to the 8th house. The depth of your preparation and the experience gained during that time will determine how effectively you can utilize this newfound leverage for personal growth and achievement during the transit in the 9th, 10th, and 11th houses.

If you're skeptical, I encourage you to crosscheck with a Vedic astrologer to confirm this insight. Remember, Saturn takes approximately 2.5 years to transit each house, and understanding these cycles can help you manage your expectations and prepare for the right moments to leverage your skills and opportunities.

Saturn is often referred to as a taskmaster in astrology due to its association with discipline, responsibility, and structure. This planet embodies the lessons of hard work, perseverance, and the consequences of our actions, giving timely checks and rewards.

You could also track Jupiter's movements to understand potential times when luck might shine on you. Jupiter takes one year to transit each house, which equates to a 12-year cycle.

Don't sell

No, I am not talking about marketing or sales. My point is "don't sell" your pain, shortcomings, or failures.

Let me explain with an example with the help of professional wrestling, where wrestlers "sell the move." It's an act of making the opponent's offensive move appear more painful than it is. It's similar to an action movie. The dramatic flair enhances the overall experience of watching a live-action film, adding a layer of realism to the match to keep the audience engaged.

Wrestlers pull the crowd into the unfolding story by convincingly portraying pain and vulnerability, buying into the scripted violence just as they do while watching an action movie.

However, there are occasions when a wrestler doesn't "sell" the opponent's most powerful move to stand out as the toughest competitor. Instead of exaggerating the effects of a devastating blow, the wrestler will downplay it, showcasing grit and determination to push ahead despite the odds stacked against him.

This approach is incredibly relevant to our lives: we should never sell our failures to others or ourselves to draw pity or sympathy. Like a wrestler who refuses to over-dramatize their opponent's blows, we shouldn't let our problems define us or influence how we perceive our capabilities.

Accepting this mindset means recognizing our failures without letting them chip away at our confidence or push us into a victim mentality. It helps maintain:

Confidence in the face of adversity: The principle ensures confidence and composure when facing setbacks or criticism. You manifest strength and determination instead of vulnerability by refusing to "sell" your struggles or failures to draw pity or sympathy.

Regain agency over problems: Survival mechanisms kick in when we get comfortable with our mistakes, pain, and shortcomings. In other words, accepting and facing a situation and not selling problems paves the way for recovery and progress. The approach calls for individuals to take charge of their narrative and create their path.

Avoid slipping into that dangerous victim mentality: By not selling your problems, you avoid falling into a victim mentality that you and your issues are exceptional and can't be solved. This type of thinking sets the stage for a vicious road to depression, as we have discussed before in this book.

Former WWE owner Vince McMahon summed this up quite well in a two-decade-old interview with Bob Costas when asked how he would handle a potential failure of his XFL football series. McMahon stated, "I get knocked on my keister, dust myself off, and get back up. What do you mean? What impact does it have on me? I do the best I can every single day. I'm a fighter. I enjoy fighting, by the way. I like to fight. I have tremendous confidence that this is going to be a big success, but no one can expect it to be in year one."

This statement captures the essence of resilience and determination. McMahon illustrates that setbacks are simply part of the journey, and instead of wallowing in failure, he opts to learn and move forward.

The XFL may have folded in 2001 after just one season, but McMahon remained undeterred, continuing to elevate pro wrestling to new heights. (I know the serious allegations against him, but that's a different discussion and doesn't overshadow his positive side.)

Furthermore, wearing your failures, pain, and frustrations on your sleeve can be counterproductive. Just as sharks are drawn to the scent of blood in the water, manipulative people can easily sense weakness and may exploit it. So, keep your head high, handle your challenges with strength and confidence, and stay alert!

Beware of Dark Psychology

We all like to believe that our minds are under our control, but that's often not the case. Think about how many times you've walked out of a theatre feeling like a street fighter or a race car driver after watching Vin Diesel and The Rock kick butt in the Fast and Furious series.

In those moments, the adrenaline rush and excitement from the film can make you feel invincible, ready to take on the world. The action sweeps you off your feet, and you may even find yourself imagining living that high-octane lifestyle even though you know it's all make-believe.

If the media and entertainment can do that to us, imagine what covert emotional manipulation, dark persuasion, undetected mind control, and mind games can do. There are several books on dark psychology, Michael Pace's being my favourite. You can always read those and make notes.

For now, I will focus on "love bombing" and the "long con" – two methods young and old malicious individuals use to win trust, only to ultimately betray those who place their faith in them.

A malicious entity "love bombs" the target with intense, sudden, and forceful displays of affection. It creates an illusion of genuine care and connection, making the recipient feel special. This tactic is especially effective on lonely folks, all too common in today's fast-paced, often isolating world, who desperately seek attention.

Eventually, the malicious entity penetrates the target's defenses, laying the groundwork for the next stage: a shift in behavior. The attacker then withdraws the relentless and unconditional affection, expressing gratitude only when the victim exhibits the desired behavior. The sudden change leaves the victim confused and longing for the affection that was once freely given. Over time, the victim may find themselves chasing the once unconditional attention, willing to do whatever it takes to earn those fleeting moments of validation.

Imagine a young woman named Sarah who recently saw her parents' marriage fall apart. Feeling vulnerable and alone, she starts interacting with an online friend who "love bombs" her with unconditional affection and support. At first, he sends her heartfelt messages, compliments her looks, and expresses how much he enjoys talking to her. Sarah feels cherished after seeing her family life fall apart; she believes she's found someone who truly cares.

This friend's behavior drastically changes after few weeks, as the 24/7 messages of love and support taper off, leaving Sarah craving for the "love bombing" she once received. She starts neglecting other relations, putting her other priorities, including her hobbies, on hold, to focus on rekindling that initial connection. Now, the boy has established total control over the girl and can demand (literally) and get whatever he wants from the girl.

If you find yourself in a situation like Sarah's, consider testing the individual by mirroring their behavior, especially once the boy shifts away from his initial love bombing. Start by adopting a similar emotional distance and refraining from seeking their attention as usual.

He will likely respond calmly and let go if his intentions are genuine. On the other hand, if he has malicious intentions, his true nature will quickly surface as he resorts to desperate measures to regain control and manipulate the situation.

This tactic can serve as an important reality check.

The Long Con is a more drawn-out strategy, where the perpetrator invests time, energy, and money, carefully building a relationship over time to become deeply embedded in the victim's life. Once the victim feels secure and comfortable, the con artist implements the deceptive plan, causing significant emotional or financial harm.

The Tinder Swindler is an example of a long con or romance fraud. The con man, Shimon Hayut, met women on Tinder to gain their trust and steal money. He would pretend to be Simon Leviev, a wealthy man, and use a variety of tactics, including building trust through false intimacy, taking targets on expensive dates, and eventually manipulating and threatening victims.

The best way to defend against manipulative behavior is to involve elders. With their grey hairs and life experiences, these seasoned individuals often have a heightened ability to spot such entities, providing insights that you might overlook in the heat of emotional turmoil.

There are days when being aware of dark psychology tactics comes in handy. This topic reminds me of a particular experience from 2011 when my friend and I tapped into some of these tactics to ensure he wouldn't be deprived of his rightful rewards.

At the time, my friend worked as an analyst at a brokerage, providing trading recommendations involving complex derivatives strategies. Unfortunately, his immediate boss was taking advantage of his hard work by taking credit for his recommendations – after cross-checking their payoffs – effectively stealing my friend's credit.

We devised a plan when my friend confided in me about this unfair situation. We decided that my friend would become the ultimate "yes man" to his boss, setting up a sort of "long con" to earn his trust completely. The goal was to create an environment where the boss would rely on my friend's expertise without second-guessing him.

Once that trust was established, my friend recommended a flawed strategy while overlooking important risk management metrics, setting up the trade for failure. As usual, his immediate boss passed the strategy ahead under his name, but without cross-checking the details of the trade. The long con played out, and the strategy bombed, resulting in a notable loss (though not catastrophic, it was enough to leave an impact). The blame landed squarely on the immediate boss, who faced a quick demotion.

This experience underscores the importance of understanding dark psychology to safeguard your interests in competitive environments. After all, the world isn't all sunshine and rainbows!

Promises are cool but complicate life

Morality says we should always live up to our vows and promises, emphasizing integrity and trust in our relationships. Society always glorifies those who make good on promises even at the expense of their goals, happiness, and sometimes even their lives. Wisdom, however, suggests otherwise – we should think twice before making promises, as we can never truly predict how the future will unfold.

Making promises closes our eyes to changing circumstances, leading us into commitments that may no longer be feasible or appropriate. Living up to those promises can create unnecessary stress and limit our flexibility in navigating life's complexities.

Shri Krishna put it perfectly to Arjun after the latter publicly vowed to kill Jaydratha before the sunset. "The arrow, Arjun, does not strike the target; it's the archer's eye that accurately hits the mark. However, right now, your eyes are clouded by the dust of your vow. At this moment, your focus is more on the sun than the target," Krishna explained on the battlefield.

The statement emphasizes Arjuna's misguided focus, highlighting the importance of maintaining clarity of purpose rather than getting distracted by internal emotional pressures or vows.

Imagine an industrialist, X, who boasts about making record job hires in the coming months after seeing incredible profits. However, as the months roll by, the economic landscape takes a turn for the worse, and there is every possibility that X, under the pressure of his promise, will turn a blind eye to the latest adverse developments.

If he sticks to his promise to save face, he could end up hiring in a downturn, potentially driving his company into a permanent slump or the so-called "industrial sickness." The smart move would be to postpone hiring until things stabilize.

It makes sense to reconsider that promise in the light of the evolving situation. Ideally, X should have maintained flexibility from the start, communicating that hiring would depend on whether those substantial profits continue. That's what most industrialists and policymakers do, and you should, too, in your day-to-day life.

As always, pause and count to ten before making any promises. It's important to remind yourself that you can't control everything. Factors beyond your control can shift instantly, making it unrealistic and unfeasible to follow through on your commitments.

Smart folks are always aware that change is the only constant; what seems viable today may become impossible tomorrow. By making promises, we risk tying ourselves to commitments that may no longer align with reality, thereby threatening our credibility and well-being.

The other risk with promises is that they often oversimplify complex situations, leading to an unrealistic sense of certainty and security in life. Even more detrimental is the fact that promises foster dependency in others.

When we make commitments, we inadvertently place the burden of expectation on those around us. If we fail to deliver on our promises, it's not only us who suffer; it also impacts the other party, leaving them disappointed and possibly feeling betrayed.

Exercise

- Compile a list of promises made over the past five years.
- Reflect on whether you upheld those promises and consider how many impacted your time and well-being.
- Identify what prevented you from being flexible in light of changing circumstances.
- Think about ways to express intentions without making firm commitments.

The real spirituality

Gen Z is often captivated by spirituality, embracing the notion of detachment and the willingness to sacrifice all the trappings of life in pursuit of self-actualization.

However, this spiritual perspective that promotes escapism from reality is misleading.

As we've discussed before, reality can be harsh, demanding a pragmatic approach to life that stays grounded. True spirituality lies in confronting reality head-on and adapting to ensure survival and growth.

A powerful example of this can be found in the Marathi play "Tuza Ahe Tujpashi, written by the late, great P. L. Deshpande.

The play revolves around two elderly characters: one is a retired forest officer who led a wild and adventurous life, while the other is a religious preacher dedicated to promoting detachment from desires as a way of living life and mental peace. As the story unfolds, we see a fascinating ideological clash between the two. The forest officer represents a free-spirited approach to life, embracing experiences and enjoying the moment. In contrast, the preacher often appears loud and angry.

This dynamic creates a tension that highlights their differing philosophies. Throughout the play, the audience watches as the preacher becomes increasingly frustrated, despite his teachings. In a powerful climax, he ultimately breaks down, coming to terms with the shortcomings of his existence. He recognizes that while the forest officer may have lived a wild life, he embodies a greater sense of piety and detachment from worldly attachments. On the other hand, the preacher realizes that he has become overly obsessed with his frustrations.

This profound moment serves as a reminder that true spirituality and inner peace aren't simply found in the words we speak; they come from living authentically and embracing life fully. The play beautifully conveys the journey of self-discovery and the importance of acknowledging our limitations, providing a rich commentary on fulfilment and the essence of peace.

In one memorable scene that lasts about 20 minutes, the forest officer counsels his nephew, who has become enamoured with the idea of spirituality. The conversation revolves around the importance of embracing one's wants and desires, emphasizing that these experiences are meant to be enjoyed but not abused to the point they become obsessions. The latter represents an attachment that hurts life.

The forest officer shares his wisdom, explaining that life is filled with opportunities for enjoyment and fulfilment. He encourages his nephew to appreciate the beauty of his desires without letting them consume him. By acknowledging that it's perfectly normal to have wants and ambitions, he helps convey the idea that indulging in life's pleasures can coexist with a grounded perspective.

Throughout the dialogue, the forest officer's free-spirited nature shines through as he conveys the message that life is meant to be experienced fully. He warns his nephew against becoming so focused on spiritual ideals that he disregards the joys of living.

Note that Earth is fundamentally a materialistic place. Yes, you read that right. Materialism doesn't simply refer to money, cars, bank balances, properties, or assets. It encompasses everything we desire or need—

necessities, comforts, and even something as vital as oxygen.

So, when someone promotes the idea of giving up everything in the pursuit of spirituality, they may be misleading you. Embracing the material world is not inherently wrong; it's a part of our human experience. Acknowledging our needs and desires is essential to living a balanced life.

www.ingramcontent.com/pod-product-compliance
Lightning Source LLC
LaVergne TN
LVHW061559070526
838199LV00077B/7115